This book is a
special gift to you from:

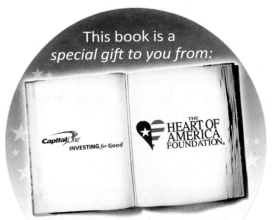

Capital One
INVESTING *for* Good

THE
HEART OF
AMERICA
FOUNDATION.

This book belongs to:

_____

The Craft of Writing

mc **Marshall Cavendish**
Benchmark
New York

Screenplays

DAN ELISH

Published by Marshall Cavendish Benchmark
An imprint of Marshall Cavendish Corporation

Other Marshall Cavendish Offices:
Marshall Cavendish International (Asia) Private Limited, 1 New Industrial Road, Singapore 536196 • Marshall Cavendish International (Thailand) Co Ltd. 253 Asoke, 12th Flr, Sukhumvit 21 Road, Klongtoey Nua, Wattana, Bangkok 10110, Thailand • Marshall Cavendish (Malaysia) Sdn Bhd, Times Subang, Lot 46, Subang Hi-Tech Industrial Park, Batu Tiga, 40000 Shah Alam, Selangor Darul Ehsan, Malaysia

Marshall Cavendish is a trademark of Times Publishing Limited

All websites were available and accurate when this book was sent to press.

Library of Congress Cataloging-in-Publication Data

Elish, Dan. • Screenplays / by Dan Elish. • p. cm.—(The craft of writing)
Includes bibliographical references and index. • ISBN 978-1-60870-501-6 (print)
ISBN 978-1-60870-653-2 (eBook) • 1. Motion picture authorship—Juvenile literature. I. Title.
PN1996.E43 2012 • 808.2'3—dc22 • 2010026164

Publisher: Michelle Bisson • Art Director: Anahid Hamparian
Series Designer: Alicia Mikles • Photo research by Lindsay Aveilhe

The photographs in this book are used by permission and through the courtesy of:
iStockphoto: cover; iStockphoto: 1; John Springer Collection/Corbis: 4; Granger Collection: 6;
SSPL/Getty Images: 7; Kobal Collection: 9; United Artists/Newscom: 14; Kobal Collection: 15:
Warner Bros/The Kobal Collection: 22; Betsie Van der Meer/Getty Images: 26; Everett Collection:
29; Kobal Collection: 34; Everett Collection: 39; Kobal Collection: 44; Everett Collection: 61, 63;
First Light: 66, 69; LucasFilm/20thCenturyFox/Newscom: 76; Glow Images: 80.

Printed in Malaysia (T)
135642

Contents

This 1894 Kinetoscope of a man sneezing, produced by the Edison laboratory, was fascinating to early film audiences.

Introduction

IN 1891, WILLIAM KENNEDY LAURIE DICKSON, an assistant in Thomas Edison's laboratory, invented the first crude motion picture projector, the Kinetoscope. A large box that stood on the floor, it allowed viewers to look through a hole to watch the first moving images. Its first demonstration, on May 20, 1891, was a three-second film called *Dickson Greeting*, which featured the inventor himself smiling amiably and tipping his hat.

Other very early films would have little more appeal to a modern audience than this one. For example, in 1894, the Edison laboratory produced a five-second film of a sneeze. Another showed a horse eating hay. Audiences of the day were thrilled; movies were new and exciting. During the early decades of the 1900s, the Kinetoscope was replaced by actual movie projectors, and theaters sprang up all over the country. By 1915, the movie business had

Screenplays

By the 1920s, the original Kinetoscopes had been replaced by movie projectors, but people still waited in line to see the original movies.

moved to Hollywood. Young actors, directors, and producers went west to make their mark.

Hollywood's first screenwriters soon learned that writing for the movies required a new set of storytelling skills. The early screenwriters—called scenarists—learned how to think visually and tell their stories using pictures, not words. Over time, the best screenplays began to have certain characteristics in common—touchstones that screenwriters could use to help them write the best possible movies.

That's the aim of this book: to introduce you—today's young screenwriter—to some basic rules of the craft that will guide you in putting your own stories down on paper. Whether you want to write a romantic comedy, a thriller, or the next great slasher flick, following good principles of screen storytelling will put you ahead of the herd and give you the best shot at seeing your own movie on the big screen.

History of Film — a Montage

YEARS BEFORE EDISON AND DICKSON'S Kinetoscope, scientists were interested in trying to make pictures move. As far back as the 1600s, a Roman inventor, Athanasius Kircher, devised a contraption called the magic lantern. With this device, when pictures painted on glass were placed in front of a lantern in a darkened room, images appeared on the opposite wall. In 1834, a British inventor named William George Horner patented the Daedalum (later renamed the Zoetrope), a device in which sequential photographs were

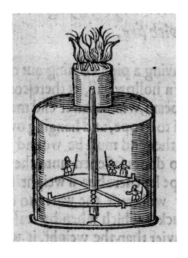

This early engraving of a Zoetrope was made for a 1635 book by John Bate called *The Mysteries of Nature and Art.*

7

lined up inside a drum. When cranked, the rotating drum gave the viewer, watching through a series of regularly spaced slits, the illusion that the pictures were moving.

After Edison and Dickson's Kinetoscope, technology soon advanced to allow moving pictures to be shown on screens in theaters. Early audiences were so enthralled with the new technology that they were content to watch practically anything. Some of these first movies recorded historic events, such as the funeral of America's twenty-fifth president, William McKinley. One early movie simply showed the director's two daughters having a pillow fight. It was only a matter of time before a filmmaker realized the new medium's incredible potential to tell a story.

> " You need to see all kinds of movies. Look at the silent ones, especially, because they had movies before they had dialogue. See how much they get across without dialogue. "
>
> —Steve de Souza, screenwriter of *Die Hard* and *48 Hrs.*

The Great Train Robbery was the first movie that told a whole story, just like a book, but, unlike any book, had live action and characters that audiences could see, hear, and almost smell.

The filmmaker who realized this potential was Edwin S. Porter, an inventor and projectionist. In 1903, his film *The Great Train Robbery* became the first to tell a story with a defined beginning, middle, and end. The movie featured gunfights, a robbery, a posse, and other elements that became standards of the Western genre. Overnight, audiences required more in the way of a plot; watching a horse eating hay or a good pillow fight was no longer enough. Movies suddenly needed stories.

Nickelodeons and Feature Films

In the first decade of the 1900s, movies (called "flickers") became the primary form of entertainment for most Americans. Movies were new, and they were also cheap. Since the first movie theaters charged only a nickel, they soon became known as nickelodeons. As movies grew more popular, newer, cleaner, and larger "movie palaces" sprang up around the country. By 1908, America boasted approximately eight thousand neighborhood theaters. Audiences came in droves to see such full-length features as *Dante's Inferno* (produced in 1911; based on the famous epic poem) and an adaptation of Charles Dickens's novel about an orphan boy turned pickpocket, *Oliver Twist* (1912). The earliest feature film that still survives intact is an adaptation of Shakespeare's *Richard III* (also released in 1912).

Who wrote these films? Early scriptwriters were often novelists or journalists looking to make extra money on the side. One of America's first screenwriters was a New York reporter, Roy McCardell, who was hired to write ten scenarios, each lasting approximately ninety seconds. He was paid $15 a script, or roughly $350 in today's money.

The First Documentary

It didn't take long for screenwriters to discover the power of sex and violence. In 1907, the first full-length documentary, *The Unwritten Law*, was released, a film that recounted the true-life tale of what many reporters dubbed the "Crime of the Century." Audiences lined up to see the movie, a dramatization of the murder of Stanford White, a well-known architect, by a millionaire, Harry Kendall Thaw, over the affections of a young showgirl, Evelyn Nesbit (who played herself).

The Star System

In the early days of film, there were no movie stars. Even more surprising, famous stage actors felt that movie acting was beneath them, something to be done on the sly for extra money. Many early American films were shot in New Jersey. Theater actors often would sneak over the river by day to make a few extra dollars starring in a picture and then hurry back to the more respectable lights of Broadway.

This suited producers just fine. The last thing movie executives wanted was for stars to become powerful and demand more money. But it wasn't long before movie fans began to identify their favorites among the actors. Since most early films didn't have credits, filmgoers of the day knew their favorite stars by descriptive names such as "the cowboy on the big horse" and "the girl on the swing."

By 1910, the most famous star of the day was the Biograph Girl, named for the company to which she was contracted. When a rival company stole her away with an offer of more money and a promise to feature her actual name in the credits, the Biograph Girl became Florence Lawrence, America's first movie star. In a matter of years, star salaries shot through the roof. By 1915, America's first big silent-film heroine, Mary Pickford, was making two thousand dollars a week, an enormous amount of money in those days. A year later, a brilliant comedian named Charlie Chaplin signed for ten thousand dollars a week. In 1919, Fatty Arbuckle became the first star to receive a million dollars a year.

Why Hollywood?

During the first decades of the movie business, Thomas Edison received a fee from the major studios for the right to use his technology to make movies. But then newer film companies realized that the farther they were from the New York area, the easier it would be to avoid paying Edison's fee. Some of the new studios set up shop in Hollywood, where they were able to avoid the detectives Edison hired to collect his money. California had another benefit: the constant warm weather was ideal for shooting movies year round.

Screenplays

Charlie Chaplin was one of the first major stars in Hollywood—and one of the few to successfully make the transition from silent film to talkies, and from slapstick comedy to drama that used laughter in order to make a serious point.

As actors' salaries skyrocketed, what happened with the screenwriters? Sometimes they didn't exist—this was the silent-film era, after all. Many films were improvised from a loose story in the director's head. In 1915, D. W. Griffith directed *The Birth of a Nation*, which became America's first feature-length blockbuster. Karl Brown, the assistant cameraman on the film, claimed that he never once saw Griffith with a script. By that time movies had existed for more than twenty years, yet even the most popular film to date had no need of a written screenplay.

Mary Pickford is known as the first female movie star, but she was also a cofounder of United Artists, a studio run by actors and directors rather than businessmen. She was also one of the originators of the Academy of Motion Picture Arts and Sciences, which we know best for the Academy Awards.

Pickfair

In 1919, Douglas Fairbanks and Mary Pickford converted an old hunting lodge in Beverly Hills into a twenty-two-room mansion with the first private swimming pool in Los Angeles. For the rest of the 1920s, Pickfair—named for its famous owners—became the center of the Hollywood social world. Dinner guests included everyone from Charlie Chaplin to the scientist Albert Einstein. After Fairbanks and Pickford divorced in 1936, Pickford lived in the house until her death in 1979. Nothing remains of the famous mansion except its entrance gates.

The Roaring Twenties

By the 1920s, America had become obsessed with film stars. Perhaps the most popular star of the day was Douglas Fairbanks, the swashbuckling star of films such as *Robin Hood* and *The Mark of Zorro*. Dubbed the King of Hollywood, Fairbanks became a founding member of the Motion Picture Academy, an organization dedicated to the advancement of the movie industry. In 1920, he married Mary Pickford. When they returned from their European honeymoon, fans turned out at train stops across the country to welcome the two stars home.

The 1920s represented the heyday of silent films. Audiences flocked to theaters across the nation to see stars; Rudolph Valentino, billed as the Latin Lover, was one of the most popular. By the end of the decade, called The Roaring Twenties, there were twenty studios churning out more than 800 films a year (these days 500 is a lot).

Then came a time that changed film history. In 1927, Warner Brothers released the *The Jazz Singer*, the first "talkie"—a film with sound—in which its star, Al Jolson, belted out the song "Mammy," for which he became famous. Audiences loved it, and studios worked frantically to churn out talkies. It wasn't long before silent stars with high-pitched voices or funny accents were replaced with new actors, often from the stage. This era is portrayed with great affection in the 1952 movie musical *Singin' in the Rain*.

Novelists Turn to Screenwriting

As the film business made the transition to talkies, some famous novelists tried their hand at writing scripts. One of the most successful was the novelist John Steinbeck, who wrote a number of films, including *The Forgotten Village* (1941) and *Viva Zapata!* (1952). The Nobel Prize–winning author William Faulkner cowrote many films, including Humphrey Bogart's *The Big Sleep* and *To Have and Have Not* (based on a novel by Ernest Hemingway). But some famous authors weren't as successful at adjusting to the new medium, where the ability to fashion a story as an accompaniment to pictures was more important than mere facility with words. F. Scott Fitzgerald may have written great novels, including *The Great Gatsby*, but he also wrote a string of long, dull screenplays.

Screenplays

The Golden Age of Hollywood

The period of 1930 through the mid–1940s, roughly the start of the Great Depression through the end of World War II, is known as Hollywood's golden age. During this period, eight major studios produced more than 7,500 feature films, more than 95 percent of the industry's films. As movies made the transition from silent to sound and then from black and white to color, Americans saw on average a film a week. The success of films gave rise to new and popular genres such as gangster films, musicals, and screwball comedies. In 1930, societal concerns about the depiction of violence, sex, religion, and crime in Hollywood films prompted the creation of the Motion Picture Production Code to set guidelines.

It is remarkable how far the movie industry came in so little time. The beginning of the sound era was marked by dialogue-heavy play adaptations, with poor acting and little or no camera movement. Quickly, Hollywood screenwriters had to learn how to move a story along with realistic dialogue. As famous playwrights, including George Kaufman (the screenwriter of many Marx Brothers' comedies), began to write for the movies, scripts became more inventive. Great stories of the day were put on film. In 1939 alone, Noel Langley, Florence Ryerson, Edgar Allan Woolf (*The Wizard of Oz*), Sidney Howard (*Gone with the Wind*), and Robert Carson (*Beau Geste*) all brilliantly adapted famous novels into even more famous movies.

The War Years and Casablanca

With the Japanese attack on Pearl Harbor in 1941, America entered World War II. Hollywood responded by forming the Office of War Information, an organization devoted to making films to support the war effort. Many classic wartime movies were inspired by the conflict. Perhaps the best was *Casablanca*, starring Humphrey Bogart as a disillusioned bar owner who is separated by the war from the woman he loves (played by Ingrid Bergman). Adapted for the screen by Julius and Philip Epstein from a play titled *Everybody Comes to Rick's* (by Murray Burnett and Joan Alison), *Casablanca*, featuring an ambivalent antihero, in-depth characterizations, and a mature look at the sacrifices individual citizens are forced to make in time of war, represented a peak in American screenwriting.

While Hollywood thrived during the war, the film business fell upon rocky times once peace was declared. After the war, actors won the right to work outside of the studio system and set their own salaries; paying these often very high salaries made it more difficult for a film to turn a profit. In addition, by the early 1950s, more than 50 percent of American homes had a television set, a new invention that cut into the movie-going audience.

The Coming of Realism

After the war, many returning soldiers got married, had families, and bought homes. Businesses thrived. But even in a decade heralded for its prosperity, seeds of the rebellion that would bloom in the 1960s could already be seen on the silver screen. Though times were good, audiences became attracted to a group of younger stars, such as Marlon Brando and James Dean, who played antiheroes—restless young men who scorned the usual social norms.

The Coming of the Blockbuster

With TV stealing more and more of the moviegoing audience, the 1960s represented Hollywood's low point. In 1963 Hollywood released only 121 feature films. Studios began to make movies overseas to save costs. Some sold off their back lots to real estate developers. In the early 1970s, MGM sold some of its most famous artifacts, including Dorothy's ruby slippers from *The Wizard of Oz*, to raise money.

The extraordinary success of two Hollywood films of the 1970s—*Jaws* (1975), written by Peter Benchley and Carl Gottlieb and directed by Steven Spielberg, and *Star Wars* (1977), written and directed by George Lucas—sent shock waves through the business. Setting records in attendance and money earned, these films convinced studios to focus on blockbusters, which were often based on material already familiar to the audience (superheroes, comic book

21

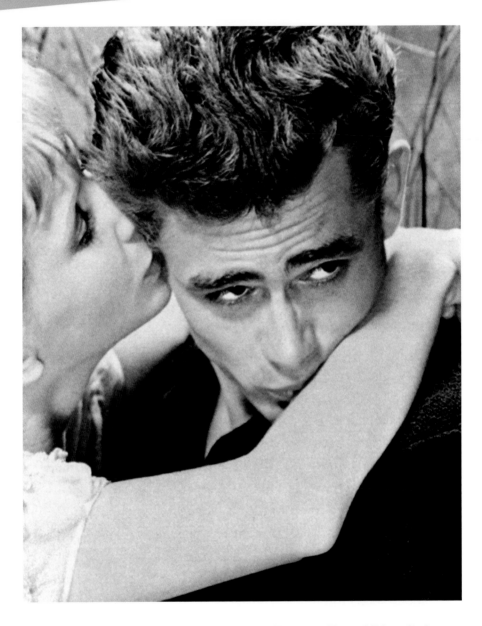

James Dean, pictured here with Julie Harris in *East of Eden*, died young but has forever been associated with the image of the restless Hollywood bad boy.

characters) and featured well-known stars. The blockbuster mentality has so transformed the industry that a movie is deemed to have succeeded or failed on the basis of how much money it makes in its first weekend in release.

Movies Today

"Nobody knows anything."

That's what the Academy Award–winning screenwriter William Goldman wrote in his famous book about the film industry, *Adventures in the Screen Trade*.

Nobody knows anything? What is that supposed to mean?

Just this: the film industry is filled with executive and creative personnel who try to figure out every day what movies the American public will want to see. The decisions they make are often a roll of the dice. At the time of their release, no one in Hollywood predicted that *Jaws* and *Star Wars* would become two of the highest-grossing films of their era. Movie executives produce films that they believe in, and then hope for the best. In other words, "nobody knows anything."

Even so, Hollywood professionals all agree that every agent and producer is looking for the same thing: a great script. A script they can fall in love with. A script they can turn into the next big hit.

So where does that leave you, the young screenwriter?

In the driver's seat. All you have to do is look into your imagination and tell your story as well as you can. Then one day, after lots of hard work, your script might well end

23

The Method

The 1950s and 1960s brought stars to the screen who were trained to delve into their own memories and emotions to create portrayals of greater realism and honesty. The Method, as this training came to be called, was developed by the Russian director Konstantin Stanislavsky and advanced in America by a prominent acting teacher, Lee Strasberg of the Actors Studio in New York City. Many of his students have acted in films over the past sixty years. Method actors who became big Hollywood stars include Montgomery Clift, Marilyn Monroe, Al Pacino, Dustin Hoffman, Robert De Niro, and more recently, Sean Penn, and Johnny Depp.

up on the desk of the right executive—a man or woman who, though overwhelmed by work, is desperately looking for a story with which they can fall in love. With any luck, the time and effort that you've put into telling that story will shine through and you'll be on your way.

It could happen. This book can help you get started.

> **You have to write a good script that gets somebody's attention. Period. If you write a good script, you'll get an agent; it's that simple.**
>
> —Jim Kouf,
> screenwriter of Rush Hour
> and Stakeout

25

One of the wonderful parts of screenwriting is sharing the process with actors and the others involved.

2 The Big Picture

SO YOU HAVE AN IDEA for a movie. Perhaps a story you've been thinking about for months or maybe even years. How do you translate the images in your head onto the page so that they form a well-written screenplay? How do you format the dialogue? What size font do you use? Do you write in the camera angles or let the director make those decisions? There are also the bigger questions, such as how to introduce your main character, how to write memorable scenes, and how to structure your overall story.

Then there's the first question you need to ask yourself, perhaps the most important of all: Is your idea really a movie?

What Are You Writing?

Sometimes the most important rules are the most basic. Even professional baseball players need to be reminded from time to time not to take their eye off the ball when they are up to bat. By the same token, before typing "FADE IN," the screenwriter needs to feel certain that the story he or she wants to tell will make a good movie. After all, some stories make better novels, short stories, plays, or TV shows. So, before you get started, give yourself a little test.

Is Your Idea Visual Enough?

Movies are stories told in a series of images. Some of the most memorable films give the director a chance to include some really juicy visuals. *Star Wars* had spaceships, weird aliens, and the Death Star. *Jaws* had that giant shark. No other medium jumps from one location to another so fluidly. If a novelist wants to switch scenes from New York to London, he or she will probably spend a couple of paragraphs describing the new scene. A playwright might have to close the curtain at the end of an act to give the backstage crew time to change the set. But a film can do it all in a single establishing shot. In a flash, James Bond is in a Porsche cruising by the Eiffel Tower. In the blink of an eye, friends who met in a bar are scuba diving off the Great Barrier Reef.

Of course, there are no hard and fast rules. By no means does your film have to include shots of the Swiss Alps and a rampaging monster. But even movies set in a single city tend to use a wide range of locales and settings to keep the viewer interested. Take *The Hangover*. Since the movie takes place almost entirely in Las Vegas, the screenwriters spiced things up by staging scenes everywhere from hotel rooms to

This scene from *The Hangover* takes place in an elevator, but in the course of the film, the characters—including the baby—really get around!

one-stop wedding chapels. In *Up in the Air*, the screenwriters Jason Reitman and Sheldon Turner move their main character across America from small towns to big cities.

Does Your Idea Fill Two Hours?

Before you start writing, make sure that your idea has enough going on to fill two hours. A story about a man talking to a friend in a bar about their childhoods might make a better short story or novel than a movie. A story that depicts the ups, downs, and moral compromises of a hardware store owner—set entirely in his shop—might make a better play. On the other hand, a story that is too sweeping in scope might not be so easily cut to two or even three hours. You might want to think twice before attempting your movie adaptation of Tolstoy's _War and Peace_ (a book that weighs in at over one thousand pages).

So, think before you start. Are your characters' problems complex enough to warrant two hours of screen time? Does your story move between different, interesting locales? Does your idea contain exciting sequences that would look really great on film—a chase up Mt. Everest on mopeds or a flaming asteroid colliding with Mars? If your answer is yes, you're off to a good start.

> " Many beginning writers make the mistake of writing a particularly popular genre without even reading the classics in that genre. "
>
> —Amy Holden Jones, screenwriter of _Mystic Pizza_ and _Indecent Proposal_

Movie Genres

Most movies that get produced today fall into a specific genre. Here are some of the most common:

Horror—movies often featuring innocent children, ax-wielding villains, and deformed monsters whose main intent is to scare the audience half to death. Examples: *The Shining*, *Friday the 13th*, the *Saw* series.

Sci-Fi—movies with spaceships, aliens, distant planets, and plots that often include an unsuspecting earthling who rises to the occasion to save the universe. Examples: *Star Wars*, *Star Trek* prequel, *Transformers*.

Fantasy—movies in which at least some of the main characters are imaginary creatures such as hobbits, elves, or talking animals. Examples: *The Chronicles of Narnia*, *The Lord of the Rings*, *Avatar*.

Romantic Comedy—movies in which the humorous elements typically involve two people—often people who seem uninterested in or even antagonistic to one another—who end up falling in love. Examples: *The Breakup, The Proposal, He's Just Not That Into You.*

Drama—movies that depict morally compromised characters grappling with a serious issue or injustice. Examples: *Kramer vs. Kramer, Platoon, Michael Clayton.*

Your Main Character

Now you're sure that your story really is a movie. So what next? Most films—in fact, most novels, plays, and TV shows—start with a main character who is placed in some sort of perilous situation and then struggles against various obstacles to get out of it. For instance, the first sequence of *The Wizard of Oz* introduces the viewer to Dorothy, a sweet girl who yearns to travel "over the rainbow." A few moments later she is torn from her comfortable, if boring, Kansas life by a giant tornado and carried to the land of Oz, where she follows a yellow brick road to the Emerald City with a scarecrow, a tin man, and a lion, all the while staying clear of a seriously angry witch. And how about Frodo in *The Lord of the Rings*? At the story's start, he is an unassuming hobbit living a simple life in the Shire. But before long, he is assigned the job of trekking to the dark land of Mordor to destroy the ring of power—no easy task (in fact, it took three movies to tell the story). In *Avatar*, Sam Worthington plays a crippled marine who is dispatched to the moon Pandora, where he becomes torn between following his orders and saving the Na'vi tribe from destruction.

These setups (and many, many more) take a main character living an otherwise unextraordinary life and place him or her in a life-or-death situation. So if you're having trouble getting started, try it yourself—it might lead you to the kind of high-stakes story that makes for a good movie.

Avatar received critical acclaim mainly due to its special effects, but without well-written characters and dialogue, this movie might have never been made.

Make Your Main Character Want Something Very, Very Badly

Of course, not every film has to put the main character in a life-or-death situation. But even if your movie doesn't transport your leading man or leading woman on a quest to save all humanity, you must give the hero something he really, really wants. Characters can yearn for love, friendship, or even a good job. In *Julie and Julia*, Julia Child doesn't just want to publish a cookbook, she's *desperate* to publish a cookbook and struggles for years to make it happen. In *Star Wars*, Luke Skywalker so badly wants to get off the small rock of a planet where he lives with his aunt and uncle that it's making him crazy. Many romantic comedies begin with a character who is desperately looking for a soul mate. In *Pretty Woman*, both Richard Gere and Julia Roberts want to find true love and are then surprised and thrilled to find it in each other.

So again, before you start writing, ask yourself, what does my character want? Does he or she want it badly enough? If you aren't sure, it's probably smart to rethink your premise. Desperate characters make for good films.

Give Your Main Character a Problem

Still having trouble getting a handle on your main character? Many scripts suffer because the hero or heroine doesn't have a big enough problem. Let's say your story is about a guy named Mark who gets in trouble with loan sharks. Don't make Mark a guy who gambles only occasionally. Make him someone who goes to the racetrack by day and the dog track by night and plays poker all weekend. Make him wake up in the middle of the night to call his bookie. Make him bet away his house.

35

Screenplays

If your story is about a woman with commitment issues—let's call her Sadie—don't make her someone who has broken up with only one or two boyfriends. Make Sadie a hopeless romantic who has dumped guy after guy after guy because none of them have measured up to her overly high standards. Have her dump a millionaire for wearing the wrong kind of shoes, a movie star for having bad breath. Then and only then have Sadie bump into Mr. Right, so that the audience can have the fun of watching her overcome her commitment issues while finally finding true love.

Most movie characters today have their share of problems. Some of the most interesting people on the screen are the most twisted. In recent years, George Clooney has made a career out of playing middle-aged men who are likable yet morally compromised. In *Up in the Air*, the audience couldn't be sure whether his character was going to make a sincere stab at connecting with another person until the end. Think of Mel Gibson in *Lethal Weapon*. Talk about a man with issues. In one of his first scenes, he weeps over his dead wife and sticks a gun in his mouth. A detective with a serious death wish, Gibson rediscovers his will to live by the end of the film.

So, don't be afraid to make your main character complicated. Give him or her a dark, haunting secret. Or a drinking problem. Or a bad history with the opposite sex. Anything. But before you start, make sure you're writing about a character who is complicated enough and wants something badly enough to sustain an entire movie.

36

The Rule of But

The film teacher Andy Stein suggests using "the rule of *but*" to create interesting characters. It works like this: When thinking through a hero's characteristics, don't think, "Ron is shy." Instead, think, "Ron is shy *but* comes out of his shell when discussing baseball." Don't think, "Susan is smart." Instead, think, "Susan is smart *but* often feels dumb when she's around men who remind her of her father." In other words, give your characters shading; make them complex. Make them real, living people.

Screenplays

The Three-Act Structure

OK, now that you know your main character, it's time to discuss a screenplay's basic structure. Let's say an average screenplay is 120 pages, with each page taking about a minute of screen time. (Another way to think of a screenplay is as a series of 60 two-page scenes.) Luckily, the best screenplays pretty much always break down into three distinct acts. It's true. Whether your script is a sci-fi thriller, a Western, or a love story, specific story beats tend to occur at the same time. Here is how it breaks down:

Act 1. In the first half hour of your movie (pages 1 to 30 of your script), it's your job to set up the basic story and introduce the main character. The first ten pages or so of *The Lord of the Rings* show Frodo living a peaceful life in the Shire, preparing to take over his uncle Bilbo's home. In *The Wizard of Oz*, Dorothy is living on her aunt and uncle's farm, where her primary concern is saving her dog, Toto, from the evil Almira Gulch. Then toward the end of the first act—say, between pages 20 and 25—something drastic needs to happen to your hero or heroine that throws his or her world completely out of whack. Frodo has to leave the Shire and destroy the ring of power; Dorothy gets swept away by a tornado to Munchkin land. By page 30 at the latest, your hero or heroine needs to set off on some sort of journey. (Frodo and Sam leave the Shire, chased by the black riders; Dorothy sets off on the yellow brick road, headed for the Emerald City.)

Act 2. The middle sixty pages, or act 2, of a screenplay contains the meat of your story. But even the best

There are many scary moments in *The Wizard of Oz*, but what makes the movie a classic is its brilliant dramatic structure.

Hollywood screenwriters can find it difficult to string together a series of scenes that take their main character convincingly from the start of his or her journey to a point near the end. Sometimes that journey is physical, as in *The Wizard of Oz*, whose act 2 shows Dorothy meeting up with a scarecrow, a tin man, and a lion, arriving

Screenplays

at the Emerald City, and setting off to capture the wicked witch's broomstick. Sometimes the character's journeys are emotional. Act 2 of *When Harry Met Sally* dramatizes Harry and Sally becoming closer and closer until they become briefly involved and Harry runs away.

To make it easier, it can be helpful to think of act 2 as having two distinct sections. During the first half of act 2 (pages 31 to 60) your character should have a specific goal. Then at the midpoint of the script—around page 60—your hero or heroine either:

a) fails and is forced to formulate a new plan that takes him or her from pages 60 to 90, or

b) succeeds only to instantly discover that there is something even bigger that he or she has to do (this turn of events also takes the story to page 90).

Often, act 2 ends with the main character in some sort of very serious peril. In romantic comedies, the main couple might break up. In a more serious film, a supporting character might die, or the main character might revert to some crippling vice or trait that he or she has tried to lick since act 1. Maybe the character becomes so distressed that he or she starts to smoke or drink or gamble. Luckily, there is act 3, where everything is resolved.

Act 3. Once you hit page 90, your story is cruising to the finish. It's time for your main character to rise to the occasion and save the day. Act 3 is where the hero finally beats the bad guys or Dorothy melts the wicked witch. In lighter movies, it's where Harry, alone and miserable, realizes it's Sally whom he really wants.

The Dark Moment

Most screenplays have a point toward the end of act 3 where it looks like the main character simply cannot win. It's the moment where Dorothy, trapped in the witch's castle, watches the sand in the hourglass nearly run out (signifying that she will be killed), only to be saved by the scarecrow, the tin man, and the lion. It's the moment in *Star Wars* where Luke is about to be shot down and Han Solo returns at the last possible second to destroy the enemy ship so that Luke can destroy the Death Star. Does your movie have a "dark moment"? Most do. And yours will be better if you can find a believable way to put your main character in some sort of final peril before the dawn breaks.

Deconstructing Star Wars

The first *Star Wars* movie fits perfectly into the classic three-act structure that defines most good screenplays.

Act 1: Luke Skywalker receives a message to deliver a droid to Alderaan.

Act 2 (first section): Luke finds Obi-Wan Kenobi and Han Solo. Together, they fly to Alderaan only to discover it has been destroyed. Defeated in their first quest, they are captured by Darth Vader.

Act 2 (second section): The heroes have a new goal: escape the Death Star. Obi-Wan Kenobi sacrifices his life, and the heroes flee to safety. Or do they? The stakes grow higher when Luke and friends discover that they must destroy the dreaded Death Star before it destroys them.

Act 3: Drawing on the power of "the Force," Luke destroys the Death Star.

Do all good screenplays fall neatly into this format? The answer is almost always. There are exceptions, of course. Films such as *Pulp Fiction* and *Being John Malkovich*, in which the stories are told out of order, don't fit neatly into the basic three-act structure. But pretty much any movie in which the series of events is told in any kind of chronological order uses the same basic structure. Akiva Goldsman, the Academy Award–winning screenwriter of *A Beautiful Mind*, put it like this:

> **The first thing you have to do is learn**
> **what the body of a screenplay looks like**
> **. . . you can say something happens on**
> **page 30, something bigger happens**
> **on page 60 and something really**
> **depressing happens on page 90. And**
> **then something totally amazing happens**
> **on page 120.**

Sounds simplistic, but it works. So before you start your movie, put it to Goldsman's test. What happens to your main character on page 30? What sort of journey does he or she embark on? Then what happens on page 60 that forces your character to find a new quest or focus? Then what setback happens on page 90? Then how does your main character emerge triumphant to give an audience a satisfying ending?

It can be helpful (and fun) to break down your favorite movies in the same way. Of course, you should know your own basic plot points before you start your own screenplay.

When Harry Met Sally tells the story of boy meets girl, boy doesn't like girl, boy likes girl, boy loses girl, boy gets girl. What makes it special is the amazing repartee crafted by screenwriter Nora Ephron.

3 Things to Think About

NOW THAT YOU'VE THOUGHT ABOUT your main character's journey through the three acts of a screenplay, it's time to get more specific. How do you write a good scene? What makes good dialogue? What are some of the best ways to get your movie off on the right foot? Then there's the most basic question of all: How do you make your script look professional?

Most Hollywood agents are deluged with scripts. So most judge a new writer's screenplay by its first ten pages. Scott Rosenberg, the screenwriter of *Con Air*, put it like this: "You can tell from the first page if someone can write, by its assuredness and its confidence. . . . If, right off the bat, there are four-inch blocks of text, or it's not formatted properly, I know it's an amateur."

So first things first, let's make sure your script looks good—the mark of a professional.

Screenplays

The Correct Format

More than any other kind of writing, screenplays have an agreed-upon format. Here is a quick cheat sheet to get you started.

Font: Screenplays are written in 12-point Courier and start with the words "FADE IN": written in capital letters (or CAPS), flush all the way to the top left margin. All scripts end with the words "FADE OUT": flush left at the end.

Setting Your Scenes: A new scene is indicated in a screenplay with a logline that tells the reader where the scene is taking place. A logline starts with the abbreviation INT. (for an interior shot) or EXT. (for an exterior shot), followed by a short description of the setting and the time of day. A typical logline might look like this:

EXT. SANTA'S WORKSHOP—DAWN ON CHRISTMAS MORNING

Or this:

INT. A SMALL KITCHEN—NIGHT

Narration: After the logline, there usually follows a short description of the basic scene: where it is and who is in it. This description is always typed flush left to the margin. A basic rule of thumb is to keep descriptions brief and punchy. For instance, don't write, "Dave comes chugging down the street, stops to look in the window of a bookstore, scratches his foot, and then wanders into the bar while humming the opening bars of 'God Bless America'."

Instead, write, "Dave bursts into the bar." Save the page-long descriptions of a character's wardrobe for your novel. Avoid long blocks of text. Describe only what is necessary and push on with the dialogue and the action.

Introducing Characters: When first introducing a character, capitalize his or her name and include one or two pertinent details. Again, don't go on and on. Keep it short and interesting.

Dialogue: After you've introduced your characters, it's probably time to get them talking. Center character names in all CAPS and then center the dialogue underneath. Dialogue should not run all the way to the margins but should take up only about half the page. Try not to indicate your character's feelings through parentheticals under their name. For instance, you do not have to write:

LYDIA
(*furiously*)
Who stole my car?

The "furiously" isn't necessary. It should be obvious from the context that Lydia is furious.

Dialogue that is said offscreen (OS) or in a voice-over (VO) should be indicated by placing the appropriate abbreviation after the character's name. For example:

JIM (VO)
I grew up in a small town
in Ohio.

Sound Effects: When writing a narration, indicate sound effects in CAPS, as in:

```
The car overturns and EXPLODES as THUN-
DER cracks.
```

Camera Angles: Do not include them. Do not litter your script with terms such as "Cross Dissolve" and "Jump Cut." You are the writer, not the director.

When Harry Met Sally excerpt

What follows is a short example from *When Harry Met Sally*. Notice how the descriptions are short and punchy and don't tell more than is necessary.

```
EXT. NATIONAL AIRPORT—DAY
     (logline, showing where we are)
The plane lands.


INT. NATIONAL AIRPORT—DAY
     (new logline—now we're inside the airport)
Harry and Sally are on a
moving sidewalk. Harry is
several steps behind Sally. He
makes his way past the other
passengers to stand by her.
```

(Brief descriptions, only saying what is absolutely necessary)

```
                    HARRY
               Staying over?
```
(The character names are in CAPS.
Dialogue and names are centered)

```
                    SALLY
                    Yes.
```

```
                    HARRY
          Would you like to have dinner?
```

```
            Sally looks at him
            suspiciously.
```

```
            Just friends.
```

(If the character's lines continue on the next page,
it is set as HARRY (CONT.))

The First Pages

Good screenwriting depends on moving the story along and keeping your descriptions to a minimum. If you're having trouble knowing where to begin, a good rule of thumb is to start with your main character doing something active. Pick almost any popular movie. *Meet the Parents* begins with Ben Stiller's character proposing to his fiancée in front of her elementary school class. James Bond movies always begin with a wild chase. Many thrillers start with a crime. But however you choose to begin, it's your job to hook the reader.

What follows is the opening description from Peter Jackson's 2005 remake of *King Kong*.

EXT. SKIES OVER FRANCE 1917—DAY
(logline)

    CAMERA drifts towards a large
    puffy cloud floating 6000 ft
    above the French countryside
    . . . a roar of engines—
    sounding like angry buzzing
    bees—and three . . . six
    . . . NINE SOPWITH CAMEL
    FIGHTER PLANES emerge from
    the cloud, flying in tight
    formation . . .

See how the writers, Peter Jackson and Fran Walsh, start their script with a bang. From the logline, we know we're back in World War I. Then, with a few choice sentences, Jackson and Walsh get right to the story. Out of the clouds comes the "roar of engines," which sound like "angry buzzing bees," and nine planes swoop out of the sky, creating an exciting visual for the reader. After another line or two of description, Jackson and Walsh are ready to introduce their characters:

> JACK DRISCOLL and his buddy,
> MATT HAMON are flying two of
> the CAMELS at the rear of
> the formation. An UPTIGHT
> BRIT—McKECKNIE, is flying
> alongside them. He's as
> JUMPY AS HELL, scanning the
> skies for enemy planes.

Again, see how the writers make their words count. The words are few. Jack and Matt are "buddies". McKenzie is an "uptight Brit" and "JUMPY AS HELL" (capitalized so the reader is sure to notice it). And is this a pleasure flight? No. They are scanning the skies for the enemy. Right away, the movie—at least the movie as it appears on the page—is off to an exciting start.

The First Ten Pages

One of the most common problems with the first draft of a new script is that it takes too long to get going. Unless you're writing a purposely slow-paced character study, it's often smart to make sure that something striking happens to your character by page 10, a beat that is sometimes called "the inciting incident." Take the opening of *Big*. In the opening series of scenes, we see that Josh, our hero, is too little to get on the ride at an amusement park and that he's having trouble attracting the interest of Cynthia Benson, a pretty eighth grader. So what does Josh do? He comes across a carnival game called "Zoltar Speaks" and wishes that he was big, which sets off the main action of the movie.

What are some other "inciting incidents"? In *The Wizard of Oz*, it's the tornado. In *The Sound of Music*, it is when the Mother Abbey sends Maria to work at Captain Von Trapp's. In *The Hangover*, it's when the four guys head off to Las Vegas for a bachelor party.

So think about your movie. Look at page 10. Does something happen that really gets your story going? If not, you might want to rethink your beginning. Maybe you're taking too long on your set up? Don't leave the audience members squirming in the seats. They might get up for popcorn and not come back.

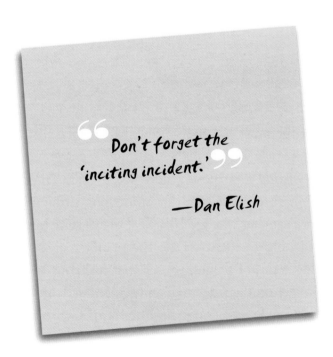

"Don't forget the 'inciting incident.'"

—Dan Elish

Dialogue

> *"A good film script should be able to do completely without dialogue."*
>
> —David Mamet, writer of The Untouchables

Without dialogue? *Really?* Well, in reality probably not. But what David Mamet is trying to get across is that at heart film is a visual medium. The best filmmakers choose images that are strong enough so that their movies can be followed with the sound off. (Next time you're on a plane, try watching the in-flight movie without the headphones.)

Even so, writers today need to write dialogue. So how do you make yours come alive? One way is to listen. Next time you're in a coffeehouse, eavesdrop on the couple sitting across the way. Notice how they don't speak in complete sentences. Notice how people tend to interrupt each other. Get a feel for the rhythm of natural conversation.

> 66 I highly recommend that beginning writers take an acting class. Be active in it, direct a scene with actors and see what animates the scene and what you can leave off the page. You can build muscles for writing good dialogue. 99
>
> —Michael Schiffer, writer of The Peacemaker and Crimson Tide

Another thing to listen for: How do people express emotions? Do they say precisely what is on their mind? Sometimes, but not always. Instead of shouting, "I'm angry with you," a person is more likely to hit the table with a fist and snap, "Get the sugar yourself!" Though it is sometimes necessary to write the big scene in which your characters express their feelings directly, one of the arts of screenwriting is being able to show the audience how your characters are feeling without making them say it. So, find different behaviors—things the viewer can *see*—to show what's going on inside. Have a nervous character rip his napkin into little pieces while he's talking. Have a kind character stop the conversation to offer an older man his chair.

Screenwriters have to learn a final trick in writing dialogue. As you eavesdrop in the coffeehouse, you'll discover that people can take forever to get across what they're trying to say. Actual conversations rarely have an elegant beginning, middle, or end. Your job as a screenwriter, though, is to make your dialogue sound as natural and unscripted as you can, while making sure not to let your scenes go on longer than absolutely necessary.

Exposition

Exposition is the background information that an audience needs to understand to be able to follow your story. In general, it's best to spoon-feed the info your audience needs by keeping your characters as active as possible. Try not to have one character simply tell another information the audience needs to know to follow the plot (also called the backstory). Avoid scenes like this:

EXT. A SUBURBAN STREET—DAY

    Nick and Joan jog side by side.

             NICK
        No! Really?

             JOAN
      Yep! Ann and Arnold just got
           divorced.

             NICK
    I thought they just got married.

Catchphrases

Some of the best screenwriters give their characters catchphrases or lines of dialogue they can repeat throughout the film. In *Butch Cassidy and the Sundance Kid*, William Goldman had Butch and Sundance repeatedly look at the posse that was chasing them and wonder, "Who are those guys?"

Come up with a phrase or two that your main character repeats periodically. It can help make your character, not to mention your script, more memorable.

                    JOAN
      True. But when Arnold got arrested
       for insider trading, Ann decided
       to get back together with her ex-
                  boyfriend.

                    NICK
      You mean the professional wrestler?
        Who got kicked out of the air
                   force?

                    JOAN
      And then spent a year in prison.

You get the point. It would be obvious to any movie-
goer that this awkward dialogue is in the script to fill in
background information. If your movie absolutely requires
a scene where the leads need to tell each other some facts—
such as police officers discussing the background of a murder case—spice it up by giving your characters interesting
quirks. Make the big detective addicted to grape lollipops.
Or put expositional but necessary scenes in unusual locales.
Have the police fill each other in on a case while cruising
the crime scene in a motorboat. Have two neighbors discuss the postal officer's past while bungee jumping.

The trick is to get that information across in quick,
interesting scenes that seem natural. For instance, how did
Noel Langley, Florence Ryerson, and Edgar Allan Woolf,
the screenwriters of *The Wizard of Oz*, get the viewer into

the story? Did they open the movie with Dorothy talking to a friend about how life on the farm stank? No, they started with Dorothy holding Toto and running down the road with the mean Mrs. Gulch hot on their heels. Then, through various interactions with the farmhands (who we find out later are the scarecrow, the tin man, and the lion), we discover without her having to say a word about it that she is unhappy. Then she sings "Somewhere over the Rainbow."

Scenes

As mentioned before, the average movie script is made up of about sixty two-minute scenes. Of course, not every scene is two minutes. The length of an individual scene obviously depends on what your characters have to accomplish in it. In any case, here are some things to keep in mind as you approach your scene work.

Enter Late, Leave Early. Most Hollywood writers say that it's best to enter your scenes as late as you possibly can and then get to the point and get out. What exactly does that mean? Well, let's say a police officer is off to interview a suspect. It is often better not to waste valuable screen time showing the police officer driving to the suspect's house, introducing himself to his wife and kids, and accepting an offer of a cup of coffee. It is better to pick up the scene with the introductions over and the cop already asking direct questions about the crime. Try and do that throughout your screenplay. If you're writing a scene where friends meet for lunch, don't show them arriving at the restaurant. Instead, have them already seated at the table in midconversation. *Star Wars* doesn't open with Princess Leia's ship coasting happily through space. It starts with the ship already under attack.

Make Sure Something Happens. Never forget that movies are meant to be entertaining. Put another way, don't forget to make sure that something interesting or funny or romantic or violent happens in every single one of your scenes. Whether it's a car crash, a murder, an absurd situation, or even a man taking his wife breakfast in bed for the first time—every scene needs to engage the audience and move the plot forward while telling the viewer something about the characters.

The Glory of the Short Scene. Some of the most effective scenes are the shortest. In *Star Wars*, there is a moment in the first act when the Imperial Raiders are looking for the small robot R2D2. The scene opens with an enemy soldier finding a footprint in the sand. He looks to his commander and says a single word, "Droids." From that five-second scene, we know that the good guys are in serious trouble. In *Julie and Julia*, Julia Child, played by Meryl Streep, tells her husband that her sister is pregnant. She then starts to cry and says, "I'm so happy." With a great actor and a few lines of dialogue, Nora Ephron, the screenwriter, shows the viewer how badly Julia wants her own baby and how conflicted she is about her sister's good news.

Of course, some scenes warrant a healthy chunk of screen time. But a basic rule of thumb is that a scene that runs more than two or three pages had better have a lot

Upping the Stakes

Many movies start off with an ordinary character who is thrust into some sort of strange situation. If your script has this element, you're off to a good start. Now it's your job to up the stakes to make things as difficult as you can for your main character before he or she emerges triumphant in the end. Take *Jaws*. At the start of the picture, Brody (played by Roy Scheider), is a small-town police chief. By the end, he is fighting off a giant killer shark.

In *Back to the Future*, Marty McFly (Michael J. Fox) travels twenty years back in time and finds himself in his hometown. The writers then raise the stakes. First, Marty's mother (who is a teenager) falls in love with him. Then Marty realizes that if his parents don't hook up at a certain dance, he'll never be born!

See if you can do the same thing. Twist your premise so your characters get in as much trouble as you can devise—then and only then, let them find some sort of resolution.

In *Back to the Future*, Marty McFly ends up ensuring that his parents become a couple—so that he can be born twenty years later. It's a great example of fun science fiction writing.

happening. Save your long scenes for when the two main characters finally admit that they love each other or when the good guy and bad guy finally have a showdown.

And finally, if you aren't sure how you want a scene to go, try it different ways. The screenwriter Richard Curtis (*Four Weddings and a Funeral* and *Notting Hill)* sometimes writes five possible versions of a single scene and then uses the one he likes best. If a scene isn't working, it probably isn't necessary. Don't get bogged down. Move on and come back to it later. It's possible that after working ahead in your script, you'll be able to see an old scene with fresh eyes.

Supporting Characters

Obviously, every movie needs more than an interesting main character. Your hero or heroine is going to need a supporting cast. Dorothy had the scarecrow, the tin man, and the lion. (She also had Toto.) Butch Cassidy had Sundance. Luke Skywalker had Obi-Wan Kenobi, Han Solo, Princess Leia, and two droids.

While some supporting characters serve as mentors or teachers (Obi-Wan Kenobi), others might represent the darker side of the hero (Han Solo) or serve primarily as the comic relief (the British droid 3CPO). However your supporting characters function in the script, try to make them all interesting; give each one a few unique quirks. In the *Stars Wars* movies, the writer/director George Lucas turned the traditional wise old man into Yoda, a strange alien with unusual syntax. He gave the tough guy, Han

The Joker in *The Dark Knight* is one of the scariest characters ever written!

Solo, a refreshing sense of humor. The maiden in distress, Princess Leia, turned out to be tougher than virtually anyone else on-screen.

And while you're creating a great, quirky cast of supporting characters, don't forget to make a really interesting antagonist (a fancy word for the bad guy). Remember: it is often the villain who drives the action of the movie. James Bond doesn't go out on a case for the fun of it. He goes because there's a maniac on the loose intent on destroying the world. For the audience to be impressed with Luke Skywalker's heroics, it has to believe that he is up against a worthy opponent, someone truly terrifying. Meet Darth Vader. Bad guys often set the wheels of the plot in motion. As noted, *Star Wars* opens with Darth Vader boarding a ship. In *The Dark Knight*, Batman defends Gotham City from a seriously strange bad guy: the Joker, played by Heath Ledger.

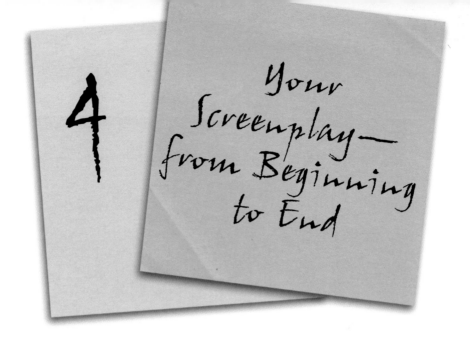

4

Your Screenplay— from Beginning to End

SO, IT'S FINALLY TIME to start writing. Perhaps you can't wait to put words down on paper and whip off the first draft. Or maybe you still feel unsure about how to get started. Before you fire up your laptop, here are a few suggestions on ways to make it easier to confront the blank computer screen.

Getting an Idea

It may seem obvious, but half the battle of writing something great is having a great idea. Of course, that's easier said than done. The screenwriter Jim Kouf has said, "The toughest thing is to keep coming up with original ideas. You have to go through a hundred ideas to find the one that's right. That takes a lot of thought and a lot of trying. You just keep writing."

If you're having trouble finding the right story to tell, a good way to start is to make a list of your favorite

Everything starts with an idea—the light bulb inside your mind!

movies. Then stick them in your DVD player and study how the writers structured the stories. Let the work you love inspire you. Don't be afraid to think something like, "Hmmm . . . I loved *Avatar* and *X-Men*, but . . . maybe I could write something just as good." No maybes—you can! With your favorite movies in mind, brainstorm your own plots. Then take your best ideas and ask some basic questions. Does your story have a strong main character who wants something very badly? Are there a varied set of supporting characters? Is there an obvious act 1 break where the hero embarks on some sort of journey? Can you figure out the main plot points and how they fit into the three-act structure? And finally, and perhaps most important, is the idea something you love? Something you think that you can write well?

If the answer is yes to all of the above questions, then you're ready. Time to move on to your outline.

> " I always carry a bunch of three-by-five cards where I write ideas that come to me, bits of dialogue, or odd observations. Eventually, a couple of them will collide to form a whole new idea or they will achieve a critical mass and a lit bulb will flash in my head and I'll say that's a story. "
>
> —Steve de Souza, writer of Die Hard and Running Man

Screenplays

Twelve Sequences

As mentioned earlier, some Hollywood screenwriters like to think of movie scripts as sixty two-page scenes. Similarly, you can break your movie down to twelve ten-page sequences. (A sequence is a section of a film that has the dramatic continuity to almost stand on its own. An extended car chase can make up a sequence. The final attack in *Star Wars*, in which Luke ultimately blows up the Death Star, is another sequence). With each sequence lasting around ten minutes, the first three make up the first act (the first thirty minutes of the film). The middle six sequences make up the second act (thirty to ninety minutes), and the final three sequences make up the third act (ninety minutes to the end).

While it isn't absolutely necessary, it can be helpful to break your script into these twelve ten-minute parts. Then figure out what major plot point happens at the end of each ten-minute section. For instance, the end of the first sequence should be where the first strange thing—or "inciting incident"—happens to your main character. But what is happening to him or her after twenty minutes of your movie? How about after thirty? (That should be the end of act 1, where your main character starts off on his or her journey.) If you can figure out what is happening to your main character at these twelve points in your script, you're a long way down the road to being able to fill in the scenes that get him or her from point A to B and then from B to C.

How do you learn how to write movies? Watch watch watch watch watch them. And then take notes.

Screenplays

Brainstorm Scenes

Some writers use note cards. Some scribble scenes on a piece of paper. But at a certain point, it makes sense to jot down a sentence-long description of every scene in your movie and then try and put them in order. Just keep it simple. The opening scenes of *The Wizard of Oz* might read something like this:

```
Dorothy runs toward her aunt and
uncle's farm, worried that Toto
will be taken by Mrs. Gulch.

Dorothy interacts with the
farmhands and falls into the
pigpen.

Dorothy sings "Somewhere Over
the Rainbow."
```

Again, keep track of your overall structure. Does something memorable happen to your character on page 10? Is he or she off on some sort of journey by page 30 at the latest? How does it all resolve? What's your hero or heroine's "dark moment"?

Once you've brainstormed a bunch of scenes (feel free to jot down well over sixty), put them in order. Then . . . well, it's finally time to write.

It's All in the Title

When you reach the point of trying to get an agent to represent your screenplay, it really helps if your script has a title that hooks the reader before he or she has even had a chance to read "FADE IN." The best movie titles tend to be short and to the point. Think about *Jaws* or *The Hangover*. Better yet is the title of a few choice words that gives the Hollywood reader an idea of what your script is about. Think about titles such as *Star Wars* and *Wedding Crashers*. In general, avoid long titles. If you are thinking of naming your movie *How the Chicken and the Duck Couldn't Find a Way to Share the Coop*, you might want to reconsider. Try *Poultry Wars*.

Screenplays

Getting to Work

Screenwriting can seem deceptively easy. After all, a novelist is responsible for letting the reader know every single thing about his characters and story. But a screenwriter can leave some things out. A screenwriter doesn't have to go into great detail about what his or her characters are wearing because the costume designer will take care of that. Nor does a screenwriter have to waste time on long physical descriptions of each character. Usually, a character will look like whatever actor is cast to play the part.

Even so, like any piece of writing, getting it right usually takes hard work and multiple rewrites. It's one thing to get some words down on the paper. It's quite another to make sure your story is correctly structured, your characters are original, and your dialogue is fresh. While it's true that Sylvester Stallone wrote the first draft of *Rocky* in a weekend, most writers take a long while to get down a first draft. But remember: no one has to see what you've written until you want them to. As Nicholas Kazan, the screenwriter of *Matilda*, put it, "You should be able to write a terrible first draft. I used to think of my first draft as simply laying out the territory, and that all the work was done in rewriting."

So let your first draft be where you spew out your ideas. Get words down on paper. Don't worry if it's messy or if all of your plot points aren't in the right places. As Kazan said, screenwriting is about rewriting. With a messy first draft down on paper, you'll be able to take a hard look at your script, cut what doesn't work, rewrite bad dialogue, and add some great new scenes.

Messy first drafts lead to good second drafts. Good second drafts lead to fantastic third and fourth drafts. So, be patient with yourself. Don't get discouraged if your first draft isn't perfect. It's not supposed to be.

> " The truth is that writing is rewriting. I am by no means the first person to say this, but let me be the latest. And I go over and over and over, scene by scene, then act by act, then sequence by sequence, until it's as tight and clean as I can possibly make it. "
>
> —Akiva Goldsman

I've Written a Decent Draft; Now What?

Some writers like to show their work to trusted friends and teachers after their first draft is completed. Others put the first draft in a drawer for a few weeks before taking a shot at a rewrite, without getting any comments. It's up to you. But at some point, it's wise to take a deep breath and show your script to people you trust. Be careful, though. Make sure your readers know a thing or two about screenplays or at least love movies. And don't show your script to just one person. A single reader might say something that leads you to a rewrite that makes your script worse instead of improving it. If you're going to show it at all, have at least three to five readers. That way, you'll have enough opinions to get a good sense of what is working and what isn't. If one out of five people tells you he or she is offended by a scene, keep it the way it is. If all five say they are offended, you'd better change it. Also, it can be helpful to join a writing workshop where you can get reactions to your material from other aspiring screenwriters. Remember: Be careful! Classmates aren't always right. Listen carefully and then use only the most helpful comments.

Troubleshooting Your Script

Obviously, as you get comments from your readers, keep the basics in mind. Most unsatisfying scripts suffer from the same set of problems. If your screenplay isn't getting the rave reviews you feel it deserves, here's a quick guide to some common problems and how to fix them.

The first act is too long. Many scripts suffer because the writer takes too long to get the action going. If something isn't happening to your character by page 10, you could be in trouble. You might need to compress the events you've dramatized to get into the meat of the story more quickly. If your first act runs more than thirty pages, your script is probably going to be considered a slow read. As Eric Roth, the writer of *The Insider* and *Forrest Gump*, has said, "The one thing I notice about bad scripts is that there's too much exposition. People talk too much and tell you what you've already seen."

Act 2 is unfocused. Some scripts suffer because the middle seems aimless, as though the writer isn't sure how to move the story toward its conclusion. Remember that it can be very helpful to think of act 2 as having two distinct sections. If your second act seems unfocused, concentrate on how your main character travels from page 30 until the midpoint. What is his or her goal? What happens at the midpoint that ups the stakes?

Act 3 is too short. Some writers are so happy to reach the end of the script that they rush the big finish. Don't. If you've set up your story well, your audience will want to see that big scene where the good guy finally wins. Again, think of the final battle scene in *Star Wars*. George Lucas doesn't have Luke Skywalker zoom in and destroy the Death Star on his first try. No, the battle is drawn out until Luke is the only one left. Only then, with a little help from Han Solo and the Force, is Luke able to save the day.

Once the deed is done, the movie comes to a quick conclusion. There is no long party scene where the heroes congratulate one another. There is no scene where Luke finally confesses his undying love for Princess Leia. Rather, there are two very short scenes: one in which Luke lands back at the base, and another where the heroes receive medals. Then the credits roll. Don't give the audience a rip-roaring final showdown only to have them sit back in their seats and wonder "When is this movie going to be over already?"

Star Wars is so absorbing it's hard to remember that the whole is made of its parts, but if you study the screenplay, you'll see its carefully honed three-act structure.

The dialogue is dull. As mentioned before, writing good dialogue is a matter of attuning your ear to your characters and how people speak around you. If your dialogue seems flat, maybe you don't know your characters well enough. Maybe your scenes go on too long. So, look at each scene and see what lines you can cut. Then revisit your characters. How do they talk? Are you capturing their personalities in their speech? Rethink and rewrite.

Making It in Hollywood

OK, you have your script. Now what do you do with it? Well, if you think what you've written is good enough to test the treacherous waters of Hollywood, you'll want to send it out to agents or production companies. But first, think if you know anyone in any kind of job in the film business. Maybe your buddy on the soccer team has an aunt in development at Dreamworks. Maybe your mom or dad went to second grade with a guy who's now a famous film editor. Maybe you're lucky enough to live in Los Angeles, where every other person you meet has some sort of job in the business.

These contacts can help. Like any other business, who you know can help you get that first big break. So don't be shy. If you know someone who works in the movie business, ask him or her to read your script or forward it to someone who will. Find out if your friend knows anyone who is looking for a screenplay.

If you don't have any contacts—or even if you do—go to the Internet and print out a list of the different studios

> "Everyone knows someone who knows someone who knows an assistant. If your script is truly great, it will rise to the top because there's so little great writing out there."
>
> —Akiva Goldsman

and agents and what kind of material they are looking for. Then send out your script with a short letter that tells the reader who you are in a sentence or two. Don't go on and on about yourself. Just supply a few relevant facts, such as your name and address, any writing credentials you may have, and a brief description of your screenplay. Then wait. If you haven't heard anything after three weeks or a month, follow up with a phone call. You'll be surprised. Yes, Hollywood players are busy, busy, busy. But they are also desperate to get their hands on the next big thing. If your premise sounds interesting enough, you may get your script read.

How to Submit a Script

While agents and producers care most about the content of scripts, presentation does matter. A few warnings:

Make sure to spell-check your letters, as well as your script. Nothing turns off an overwhelmed agent more than a cover letter that is riddled with typos.

Standard practice for presenting screenplays is on three-hole paper with brass brads fastened on the top and bottom holes.

Your title page should contain your title, name, and contact information. Absolutely nothing more. Never date your script. (You don't want a producer to think it is old). Do not include scene numbers in your screenplay. Scene numbers are put on production drafts before filming.

How do you get to Hollywood? Work hard!

Final Thoughts

Every year, hundreds of young screenwriters move to Hollywood to try to make it in the film business. Many don't succeed. But each year, there are some who do. So how do you become one of the lucky few? In truth, luck has very little to do with it. Screenwriters today break into the business the same way they did years ago and the same way your grandchildren will have to do it: They write a great script. It's that simple. Over the years, studio executives have come to be thought of as overpaid party-goers who do nothing more than take expensive lunches and attend wild parties. While it is true that a career in the movie business does come with its share of perks, most executives are hardworking, nose-to-the-grindstone types who love films. If you write a witty, dramatic, well-structured screenplay that has an original premise, the next script that they love might just be yours.

So what are you waiting for? Get to work.

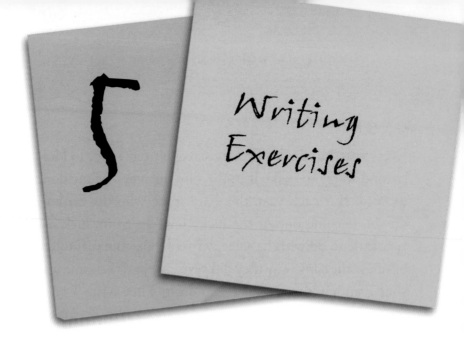

5 Writing Exercises

SOMETIMES IT'S HARD TO get your creative muscles moving. If you're having trouble getting started on your daily writing, here are some exercises you can do to get the juices flowing.

1. Watch your favorite movie. Then watch it again. Write down your favorite scenes. What makes them work? Notice how something dramatic happens in each one. Study the screenwriter's dialogue and how he or she develops characters.

2. Take a simple scene, say a man proposing to his long-term girlfriend, and write five different versions, each in a different setting. How does the scene change? Write the scene a final time but make the characters eighty years old.

3. Screenwriters have to become adept at "pitching" their stories to development heads and producers. Can

you describe your movie so it sounds as entertaining as possible in two minutes? How about in one minute? Pitch your movie to a friend. See what your friend thinks.

4. Take your favorite movie and break its major plot points into the three-act structure (inciting incident, first act break/start of act 2; midpoint, start of act 3; dark moment, coda). Then do the same thing for your idea.

5. Download a copy of one of your favorite screenplays. (Do a Google search: there are sites where you can download screenplays for free). Study the format carefully; then make sure that your script is formatted correctly. Look like a pro the first time out.

6. Get to know your characters. What does your hero like? Where did he grow up? What are his quirks? His failings? His strengths? Write a list as long as you can; then do the same for the other major characters in your script.

7. Make a list of the scenes in your movie. Does something interesting happen in each one of them? Cut the ones that seem dull and brainstorm better ones. Make an ordinary scene more memorable by placing it somewhere unusual.

8. Give yourself fifteen minutes. Write a two-minute scene in any genre between two characters that has witty dialogue and some sort of action in it.

Chapter 1

p. 8, "You need to see all kinds of movies . . .": Karl Iglesias, *The 101 Habits of Highly Successful Screenwriters*, Avon, MA: Adams Media, 2001, 29.

p. 23, "Nobody knows anything . . .": William Goldman, *Adventures in the Screen Trade*, New York: Warner Books, 1983, 39.

p. 25, "You have to write a good script . . .": Iglesias, *The 101 Habits of Highly Successful Screenwriters*, 169.

Chapter 2

p. 30, "Many beginning writers make the mistake . . .": Karl Iglesias, *The 101 Habits of Highly Successful Screenwriters*, Avon, MA: Adams Media, 2001, 30.

p. 43, "The first thing you have to do . . .": Iglesias, *The 101 Habits of Highly Successful Screenwriters*, 52.

Chapter 3

p. 45, "You can tell from the first page . . .": Karl Iglesias, *The 101 Habits of Highly Successful Screenwriters*, Avon, MA: Adams Media, 2001, 121.

pp. 48-49, "Staying over?": Nora Ephron, *When Harry Met Sally . . .*, New York: Knopf, 1996, 23.

p. 53, "A good film script . . .": David Mamet, http://thinkexist.com/quotes/david_mamet/, 1.

p. 54, "I highly recommend that beginning . . .": Iglesias, *The 101 Habits of Highly Successful Screenwriters*, 32.

Chapter 4

p. 65, "The toughest thing is to keep . . .": Karl Iglesias, *The 101 Habits of Highly Successful Screenwriters*, Avon, MA: Adams Media, 2001, 77.

p. 67, "I always carry a bunch . . .": Iglesias, *The 101 Habits of Highly Successful Screenwriters*, 50.

p. 72, "You should be able to write. . . .": Iglesias, *The 101 Habits of Highly Successful Screenwriters*, 104.

p. 73, "The truth is that writing is rewriting . . .": Iglesias, *The 101 Habits of Highly Successful Screenwriters*, 108.

pp. 74–75, "The one thing I notice about . . .": Iglesias, *The 101 Habits of Highly Successful Screenwriters*, 121.

p. 78, "Everyone knows someone who . . .": Iglesias, *The 101 Habits of Highly Successful Screenwriters*, 164.

Further Information

Books

Field, Syd. *Screenplay*. New York: Dell, 1979.

Hamlett, Christina. *Screenwriting for Teens: The 100 Principles of Scriptwriting Every Budding Writer Must Know.* Studio City, CA: Michael Wiese, 2006.

Press, Skip. *The Complete Idiot's Guide to Screenwriting*. Indianapolis, IN: Alpha, 2004.

Ury, Allen B. *Secrets of the Screen Trade*. Los Angeles: Fade In, 2005.

Websites

The History of Film
www.filmsite.org/filmh.html

The Internet Movie Database
www.imdb.com

Movie Reviews
www.RottenTomatoes.com

Read Real Scripts
www.script-o-rama.com or www.simplyscripts.com

Screenwriting Advice
www.screenwriting.info/
www.oneofus.co.uk/index.php/how_to/

All websites were accurate and accessible as of September 15, 2010.

Bibliography

Berg, Scott A. *Goldwyn: A Biography*. New York: Knopf, 1989.

Buzzell, Linda. *How to Make It in Hollywood*. New York: Harper Collins, 1996.

Ephron, Nora. *When Harry Met Sally*. New York: Knopf, 1996.

Field, Syd. *Screenplay*. New York: Dell, 1979.

Goldman, William. *Adventures in the Screen Trade*. New York: Warner Books, 1983.

Iglesias, Karl. *The 101 Habits of Highly Successful Screenwriters*. Avon, MA: Adams Media, 2001.

Langley, Noel, Florence Ryerson, and Edgar Allan Woolf. *The Wizard of Oz*. New York: Dell, 1989.

Seger, Linda. *Making a Good Script Great*. 2nd ed. New York: Samuel French, 1994.

Ury, Allen B. *Secrets of the Screen Trade: From Concept to Sale*. Los Angeles: Fade In, 2005.

Index

Page numbers in **boldface** are photographs. Proper names of fictional characters are shown by (C).

Screenplays

About the
Author

DAN ELISH is the author of many books for readers of all ages. He has also written numerous screenplays, as well as scripts for television shows, including *Cyberchase* and *Wonder Pets*. Most recently, he has completed the novel version of the upcoming movie, *The Family Hitch-cock*. He is also the author of *Fiction* and *Plays* in the Craft of Writing series, as well as many other titles for Marshall Cavendish Benchmark. Dan Elish lives in New York City with his wife and two children.